Contents

All the words that appear in **bold** are in the glossary on
page 30.

Feel the heat

All plants and animals need heat to keep them warm and alive. Heat is produced in many different ways: when things burn or rub against each other, or even when garden rubbish rots. We feel heat travelling to us from the sun, across millions of kilometres of space, or across our living room from a fire. When we are cold, a hot drink spreads welcome heat through our bodies, but in hot weather the ground can sometimes burn our feet. We need heat, but it can also be dangerous.

Can you trust your senses?

Warning! Ask an adult to pour out the hot water for you. Be careful not to scald yourself.

1 Put some hot water from the tap into a bowl. It should be as hot as you can easily bear.

2 Put cold water into another bowl. Add ice if you can.

3 Mix cold and hot water in a third container, to make lukewarm water.

4 Hold one hand in the ice cold water and the other hand in the warm water for 30 seconds.

5 Now put both hands in the lukewarm water.

Which hand feels warm?

Which feels cold?

Your body is good at judging temperature roughly. Compared to the icy water, the lukewarm water is warm.

However, compared to the hot water, the same lukewarm water felt cold, so your senses were fooled.

Thermometers

Thermometers come in all shapes and sizes. In most thermometers, the **liquid** in the tube gets bigger, or expands, as the temperature rises. Temperature is measured in equal steps called degrees, on a scale called the **Celsius** scale.

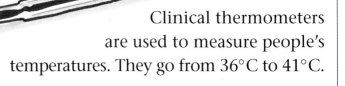

Clinical thermometers are used to measure people's temperatures. They go from 36°C to 41°C.

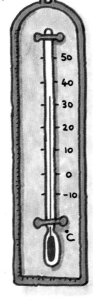

Most room thermometers go from -10°C to 50°C.

Cooking thermometers go from -10°C to 230°C.

Liquid crystals change colour with the temperature. Each number is made from a different type of crystal.

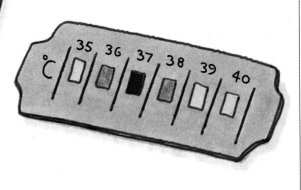

Use a thermometer to measure the temperature in different places.

What is the highest temperature that you can find?

Where can you find very low temperatures?

Warning! Do not put a room thermometer into very hot water, flames, or into an oven. The liquid inside the thermometer will expand too much and break the glass.

Did you know?

The hottest temperature ever recorded for a place was in Libya where it was 58°C in the shade.

The coldest temperature was recorded in the Antarctic. There the temperature plunged to -89°C.

Most people feel comfortable in temperatures of around 25°C.

Make your own thermometer

Do this activity over a sink and wear an apron.

You will need:
◆ **a small glass bottle** ◆ **water coloured with food colouring**
◆ **Plasticine** ◆ **a plastic straw**

1 Fill a small bottle to the brim with coloured water.

2 Put the plastic straw into the water.

3 Seal the top of the bottle with the Plasticine.

4 Press the Plasticine down so the coloured water rises up the straw.

Thermometer liquids
Liquids expand when they get warm. That is why water rises up the tube in a hot room. Factory-made thermometers are filled with alcohol or mercury, which is a liquid metal. Mercury and pure alcohol are poisonous.

5 Tape a piece of card to the bottle. Mark on it the level of the water in a cold room.

6 Do the same in a warm place. (Do not stand the bottle in boiling water to do this activity. It is dangerous!)

Repeat the activity, half filling the bottle with coloured water. What differences do you notice about the way the water behaves?

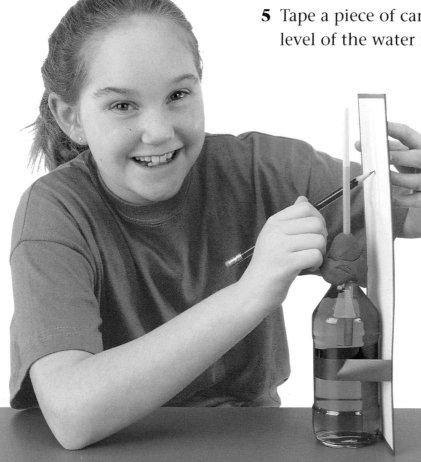

Expanding air

You will need:
- a plastic bottle cooled in a fridge
- a balloon ◆ a jar ◆ warm and cold water

1 Put a balloon over the end of the plastic bottle.

2 Put the bottle into a jar of warm water.

What happens to the balloon?

3 When nothing more happens to the balloon, put the bottle into a jar of cold water for a few minutes.

What happens now?

When the air in the bottle is warmed, it expands and stretches the balloon.

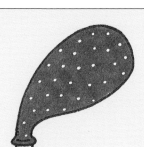

When it is cold the air shrinks, making the balloon flop.

Solids expand

Solid materials expand when they are warm. They do not change as much as liquids and **gases**.

Gap in Summer

Gap in Winter

Even so, large bridges are built on rollers so they can expand in hot weather.

Heat travels

Warning! Take care with hot water. Ask an adult to help.

You will need:

- ◆ a wooden spoon ◆ a plastic spoon ◆ a metal spoon
- ◆ a heavy container that won't tip over (such as a pan)

1 Put some hot water into a container.

2 Put the spoons into the water.

3 Which spoon's handle feels the hottest?

Which handle feels the coolest?

Conduction

Heat travels through a solid by **conduction**. Metals are good conductors of heat. Plastic and wood are poor conductors.

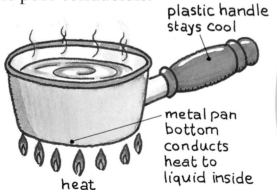

plastic handle stays cool

metal pan bottom conducts heat to liquid inside

heat

Fix metal clips to a metal spoon with wax. Which clip will fall off first after the spoon is put in hot water?

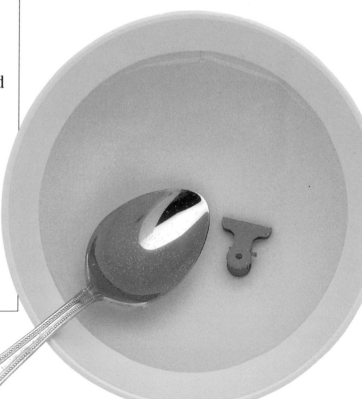

Why do some materials feel cold?

1 Feel a piece of wood. Now compare it with a piece of metal.

   Which seems warmer to the touch?

2 Touch a piece of polystyrene and compare what it feels like with a pottery cup or bowl.

Which feels the warmer? Use a thermometer to check their real temperature.

Metal and pottery conduct heat away from your hand so they feel colder than wood or polystyrene.

Hot hands

Do you think the temperature inside the glove is different from the temperature in the room around it?

Did you know?

Water conducts heat twenty-four times better than air. In very cold water, you would lose heat so quickly that you could not survive for more than a few minutes.

Penguins trap air beneath their feathers to stop heat escaping.

Seals have a thick layer of fat to stop heat conducting away from their bodies.

Heating air

Warning! Take care using candles. Ask an adult to help.

You will need:
- ♦ **an aluminium pie plate**
- ♦ **a blunt pencil**
- ♦ **some night-lights** in a tray of sand
- ♦ **Plasticine** ♦ **scissors**

1 Stick the top of the pencil into the Plasticine.

2 Carefully cut six fins into the pie plate and balance it on the blunt point of the pencil.

3 Light the night-lights and slide the tray carefully under the plate.

4 Why do you think that the plate turns?

Warning! Be careful not to set the card on fire with this activity!

Shine a strong light at the flame of a night-light standing in a tray of sand.

Hold a piece of white card behind the night-light so that you can see the shadow of the flame on it.

What happens to the air heated by the flame?

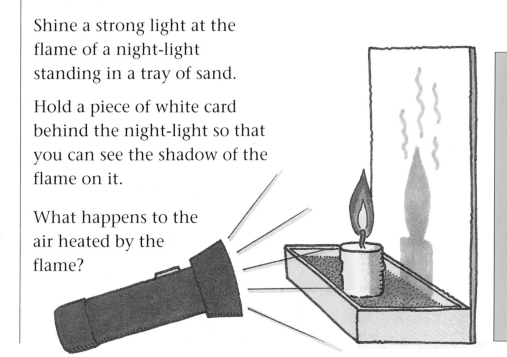

Did you know?

Mirages occur when the ground is very warm and heats the air above it. The shimmering air can look like a lake of water. You often see this effect above a road in the summer.

10

Hot and cold water

Tie string round a small bottle of warm coloured water. Lower the bottle into an aquarium or plastic tank filled with cold water. Watch the warm coloured water rise.

Did you know?

The temperature of the water at the bottom of an ice-covered pond is 4°C. Water is at its heaviest at that temperature and sinks to the bottom.

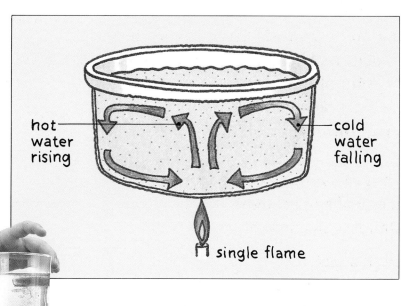

hot water rising — cold water falling

single flame

You will need:
- an ice cube made with coloured water
- a glass of warm water

Put the ice cube into the glass of warm water. Watch the cold water from the coloured ice cube sink as the ice cube melts.

11

Heat from the sun

Warning! Never look directly at the sun, and certainly not through a **lens**, or you will damage your eyes.

You will need:
- ◆ a strong magnifying glass or lens
- ◆ an old newspaper ◆ a metal tray
- ◆ a sunny day

Warning! Ask an adult to help.

1 Put the newspaper on to the tray.

2 Hold the lens so that it makes a very bright spot of light appear on the newspaper. Repeat this in different places.

3 Is it easier to scorch the black print or the white paper?

Trapping the sun's heat

1 Stand a large glass or plastic jar upside-down in the sun. Put a ther- mometer under the jar. Put another on the ground next to it.

2 Look at the temperatures of the two thermometers after ten minutes.

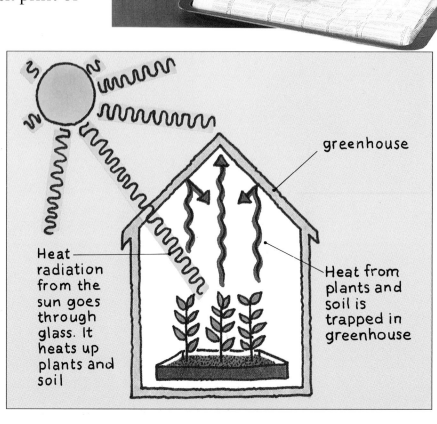

greenhouse

Heat radiation from the sun goes through glass. It heats up plants and soil

Heat from plants and soil is trapped in greenhouse

Solar cooker

You will need:

♦ card ♦ foil ♦ sticky tape ♦ wire ♦ a clean, fresh, cooked sausage ♦ a hot sunny day

1 Cover the card with foil.

2 Bend the card so that the two ends curve inwards. Use sticky tape to hold the curve in place.

3 Point the card at the sun. Use a thermometer to find the hottest place in the cooker.

4 Hold the cooker steady and try to warm up the sausage!

How it works

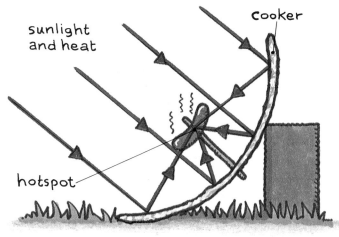

sunlight and heat

cooker

hotspot

The curve focuses the heat from the sun.

Did you know?

Inside the sun, the temperature is 15 million°C.

The temperature at the surface of the sun is 6,000°C.

Sunspots are cooler areas on the surface of the sun.

Heat travels through empty space at the speed of light.

The temperature at the surface of the planet Venus is 460°C.

Its thick carbon dioxide atmosphere traps heat.

Uranus is far away from the sun. Its surface temperature is -216°C.

Absorbing heat

Which colours absorb heat the best?

You will need:

♦ 2 thermometers
♦ black and white paper

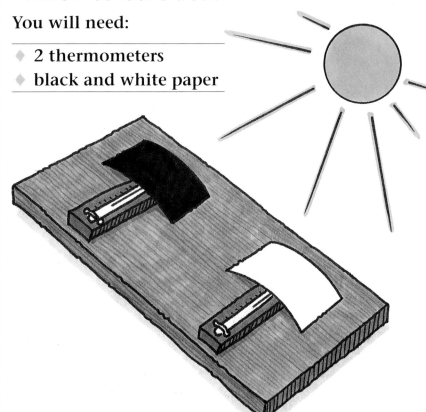

1 Put the thermometers on a sunny window sill.

2 Cover the bottom of one thermometer with white paper. Cover the bottom of the other with black paper.

3 Is there any difference between the two temperatures after half an hour?

Try covering the thermometers with other materials to see which absorb, or take in, heat the best.

You could use:

● different coloured materials
● shiny and dull materials (for example, foil and newspaper)

Survival

Shiny materials such as foil absorb heat badly, but they **reflect** it well. When people are rescued from the cold sea or from freezing mountains, they are wrapped in shiny foil blankets. These reflect the body's heat back and do not **radiate** it away.

14

Which materials absorb heat the best?

You will need:
- a tray of water
- a tray of soil
- 2 thermometers

1 Put both trays on a sunny window sill.

2 Record the temperature of the trays every 15 minutes. Do they both warm up at the same rate?

3 Make a graph of your results.

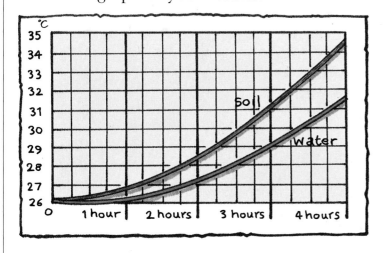

All the same temperature

1 Measure the temperature of:
- a cup of warm water
- a cup of cold water
- the room

2 After 2 hours, do the same again. You will find that they are all at the same temperature.

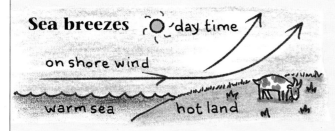 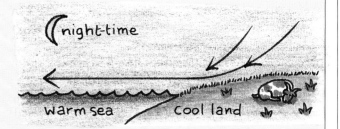

During the day, the land heats up more quickly than the sea. The air above the land grows warm and rises, so colder air from the sea blows inland into its place.

At night the sea stays warm and the land cools. This time the air over the sea rises, so the breeze blows out to sea.

15

Staying warm

Warning! Ask an adult to help you when you are using hot water.

You will need:

- ◆ **4 drinks cans**
- ◆ **a thermometer that reads up to 110°C**
- ◆ **materials such as cotton wool, foil, newspaper, fur-like fabric**

minutes	uncovered	Cotton wool	foil	fabric
0	70°C	70°C	70°C	70°C
5	62°C	66°C	63°C	63°C

1 Wrap three of the cans in different materials. Keep one can uncovered.

2 Fill each can about half full of hot water.

3 Measure the temperature of the water in each can with the thermometer.

4 Record the temperature of each can every 5 minutes. Which material keeps the water warm longest?

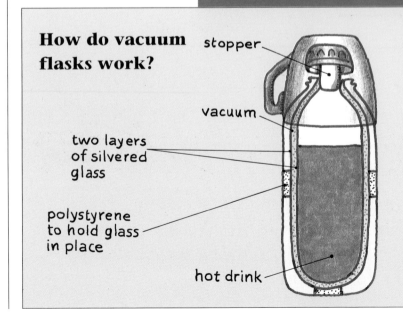

How do vacuum flasks work?

stopper

vacuum

two layers of silvered glass

polystyrene to hold glass in place

hot drink

1 The stopper stops heat escaping through **evaporation**.

2 The **vacuum** stops heat escaping by movement of air.

3 The silver layers reflect the heat back into the drink.

4 The glass is very thin so heat cannot be conducted very easily.

Do big things stay warm longer than small things?

During the Second World War, hayboxes were used in cooking to help conserve fuel supplies.

Did you know?

A large box filled with hay, or another good **insulator**, will make hot food such as stew or potatoes continue to cook, even though the food is no longer being heated up.

This happens because hardly any of the heat from the stew gets out of the thick insulation.

Warning! Ask an adult to help with this activity.

You will need:
- 3 bottles, identical except for their size

1 Fill each bottle half full of hot water.

2 Measure the temperatures of the bottles after 20 minutes. Which has stayed the warmest?

Cooling down

How can you keep milk cool without a fridge?

You will need:

- 2 bottles of water
- a thermometer
- a bowl
- a cloth

1 Put the bowl in full sunshine and stand the bottles in it. Half fill the bowl with cold water.

2 Put a damp cloth over one of the bottles.

3 Measure the temperature of both bottles after an hour.

A cool spot

Put a dab of water on the back of your hand. Wave your hand around. You will notice that the damp spot on your hand feels cool.

Sweating cools you

When sweat evaporates off your body, it cools you down.

When you come out of the sea after swimming, you feel cold if there is a wind blowing. This is because of the water evaporating off your skin.

Dogs cannot sweat. They pant to blow air over their wet tongue. Water evaporates off their tongue and cools them down.

Hygrometers

You will need:
- 2 thermometers ◆ a tissue
- a fan (you could use a book to fan the air instead)

1 Fasten some tissue to the ends of two thermometers.

2 Wet one of the tissues and keep the other one dry.

3 What do you think will happen to the temperatures of the thermometers? Explain your idea.

4 What do you think will happen if you blow air from a fan at the two thermometers? Test to see if you are right.

Sweat doesn't evaporate when it is humid.

Humidity

Hygrometers measure the amount of water **vapour** in the air. When the air is dry, water evaporates quickly. This cools the damp tissue a lot. When the air is damp, water evaporates slowly. This hardly cools the damp tissue at all.

Fans

Fans cool you down by helping sweat to evaporate from your skin.

Many people think that fans blow cold air. How could you test this idea?

Making heat

Electricity

1 Connect a small bulb (2.5 v) and battery (1.5 v) together.

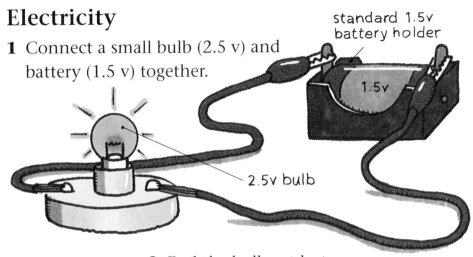

standard 1.5v battery holder

1.5v

2.5v bulb

2 Feel the bulb get hot.

The **filament** in a bulb is very thin. It glows white hot when **electricity** flows through it.

Candles

Warning! You need adult help with this activity.

1 Stand a night-light in a metal tray containing sand.

2 Carefully stick the end of a long needle into a cork.

3 Light the night-light and use the cork to hold the needle in the flame. Where in the flame does the needle glow the hottest?

Candle wax is made from chemicals called carbon, oxygen and hydrogen.

The hydrogen burns in the blue part of the flame.

The carbon burns in the yellow part.

The flame from the burning hydrogen is hotter than the flame from the carbon.

Chemical heat

1 Mix five or six spoons of plaster of Paris with water to make a thick paste.

2 Pour the paste into a margarine pot.

3 Touch the pot every 10 minutes. You should notice that it gets hot after about 20 minutes.

When plaster of Paris mixes with water, a **chemical reaction** takes place. This reaction produces heat.

Compost heaps become hot as vegetable waste is broken down by bacteria.

Green heat

1 Fill a big box with new grass cuttings.

2 Put your hand in the middle of the box to feel the temperature. Use a thermometer if you have one.

3 Leave the grass for a day or two. Now feel the temperature again.

There are **bacteria** in all living materials. When a material such as grass dies, the bacteria break it up. When the bacteria break up the grass, they release heat.

Friction makes heat

How did Stone Age people make fire?

Warning! Ask an adult to help you with this activity. Be careful not to set anything on fire when you rub the wood together.

You will need:
 ◆ **string 1 m long**
 ◆ **a bendy piece of wood or cane**
 ◆ **an old length of broomhandle or circular dowel** ◆ **a block of scrap wood dented in the middle by a hammer** ◆ **an old plastic cup**

1 Make a simple bow from the wood or cane and the string.

2 Loop the string round the dowel like this:

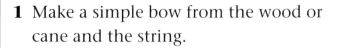

Rest the bottom of the dowel in the dent in the block.

3 Put the plastic cup over the top of the dowel and put your hand on it.

4 Move the bow backwards and forwards. The dowel should spin.

See how hot you can make the bottom of the dowel.

Flint and steel

An easier way to start a fire was to strike a piece of flint with a piece of steel.

Some lighters work in a similar way today.

steel wheel rubs against flint

wick soaked in lighter fuel

Hot tools

1 Carefully tap a large nail into a block of wood or grip the nail in a vice.

2 Keeping your fingers out of the way, saw the nail using a hacksaw.

3 When you have stopped sawing, carefully touch the side of the hacksaw's blade.

Careful! The blade will be hot!

Friction is caused when surfaces rub together. The harder they rub, the hotter they get.

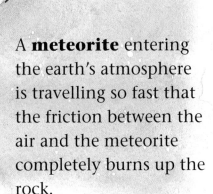

A spacecraft re-entering the earth's **atmosphere** becomes red hot. This is caused by the friction between the craft and the atmosphere.

A **meteorite** entering the earth's atmosphere is travelling so fast that the friction between the air and the meteorite completely burns up the rock.

True or false?

1 The lowest possible temperature is -20°C.
2 Big potatoes take longer to cook than small ones.
3 Only gases expand when they are heated up.
4 Penguins keep warm by having a thick layer of blubber.
5 Sunspots are cooler areas on the surface of the sun.
6 Sweating cools you down.
7 Salt water freezes at a lower temperature than fresh water.

All the answers are in this book.

23

Low temperatures

What happens when you put salt on ice?

You will need:

◆ ice cubes and crushed ice
◆ a container ◆ salt ◆ a spoon
◆ a thermometer that can measure
temperatures from -10°C to 60°C

Did you know?

The lowest possible temperature is -273°C. On the **Kelvin** temperature scale, this is 0 Kelvin. At this temperature, all gases and liquids have changed to solids. This temperature has never been reached on earth.

1 Put plenty of ice into the container.

2 Measure the temperature of the ice. It should be about 0°C.

What do you think will happen when you add salt to the ice?

3 Add about a spoonful of salt to the ice. Take the temperature a few minutes later.

What happens when you add more salt?

▲ *Spreading salt on icy roads melts the ice because salt water freezes at a much lower temperature than fresh water. Very salty water freezes at -21°C.*

24

How long does it take for ice to melt?

You will need:

♦ 3 ice cubes ♦ a thermometer with a scale from -10°C to 60°C

♦ 3 glass or clear plastic containers

♦ warm and cold water

1 Put one ice cube in water at 10°C. Put a second ice cube in 20°C water. Put the third in water at 30°C.

2 Time how long it takes for each ice cube to melt.

Put the results on a graph.

How can you make sure each test is fair?

Does it matter what an ice cube stands on?

Put an ice cube on different surfaces.

Which ice cube do you think will melt the quickest?

Explain your ideas.

How will you make sure that the test is fair?

Heating things

Solid to liquid

Warning! You will need an adult to help you with this activity.

You will need:
♦ a saucepan
♦ ice cubes
♦ a heat source such as a gas or electric ring
♦ a wooden spoon
♦ a thermometer from -10°C to 110°C

1 With an adult, put plenty of ice into a pan.

2 Slowly heat the ice. Stir with the wooden spoon. Read the temperature every minute until all the ice has melted.

3 Make a graph from your results.

Change needs heat energy

The change from ice to liquid water needs **heat energy**. While the ice is melting all the heat energy is used to change the ice to liquid. The temperature will not rise until all the ice has melted.

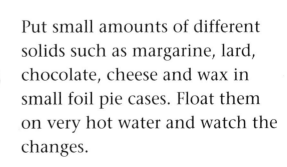

Warning! Ask an adult to help with this activity.

Put small amounts of different solids such as margarine, lard, chocolate, cheese and wax in small foil pie cases. Float them on very hot water and watch the changes.

Liquid to gas

Warning! Take great care with boiling water. These activities must only be done with an adult.

You will need:

◆ a thermometer from -10°C to 110°C
◆ a pan of water
◆ a source of heat

Find the temperature of boiling water.

Water changes from a liquid to a gas at 100°C.

High-level cookery

Did you know that water boils at a lower temperature high up in the mountains? This means that boiled food takes a long time to cook!

Quiz time

The temperature at which water boils goes down by 3°C for every 1,000 m height above sea-level.

At what temperature will water boil in towns at 5,000 m above sea-level?

The answer is on page 32.

Did you know?

Inside a pressure cooker the water boils at 115°C, so food cooks quickly.

condensed wax gas

liquid wax — hot wick

When you blow out a candle, the stream of white smoke is **condensed** wax gas. Touch this smoke with a lighted match. Watch the flame jump back to the candle wick.

Cooking

You will need:

- 2 clean potatoes of the same size
- oven gloves ◆ a metal skewer or old metal spoon ◆ an oven ◆ a fork

1 Prick the potatoes all over with the fork or the potatoes might explode in the oven.

2 Push the skewer or spoon into one of the potatoes.

3 Bake both potatoes on the same shelf of an oven for one hour at about 200°C (400°F or gas mark 6).

4 Which potato is cooked the best? What does this tell you about the way heat travels through metal?

Do small potatoes bake faster than big ones?

You will need:

- a large potato ◆ a small potato
- a fork ◆ a baking tray ◆ an oven

1 Clean both potatoes and prick them with the fork.

2 Bake them both on a tray for an hour at 200°C (400°F or gas mark 6).

3 Which potato is the softest after this time?

Potatoes cook inwards from the outside. Smaller potatoes cook faster because the heat has less distance to travel to the middle. Small potatoes also have more surface area to their volume, which can take in heat. The skewer works because the metal conducts heat into the centre of the potato.

Baked Alaska: Can you bake ice-cream without it melting?

You will need:

 ♦ a sponge-cake about 15 cm in diameter ♦ a block of vanilla ice-cream ♦ jam ♦ 3 egg whites ♦ 100g of caster sugar ♦ an oven

1 Heat the oven to about 230°C (450°F or gas mark 8).

2 Put the sponge-cake on a metal tray. (You can buy a sponge or make your own.)

3 Spread jam on top of the sponge.

4 Whisk the egg whites in a clean bowl until the mixture is very stiff.

5 Add the sugar and whisk it in to make a meringue mixture.

6 Put the ice-cream on to the sponge. Spread the meringue mixture on top, leaving no gaps at all.

7 Bake in the oven until the meringue is golden brown.

8 Eat straight away.

Sponge and meringue are good insulators. The heat can't get to the ice cream

Ice cream stays frozen

Where's the weight gone?

Weigh some cake mixture before and after it goes into the oven.

Why do you think it weighs less after it has been cooked?

Glossary

Atmosphere The layer of gases that makes up the air surrounding the earth.

Bacteria Tiny living creatures that break down waste.

Celsius The temperature scale, invented by a Swedish scientist, that takes the freezing point of water at sea-level as zero and the boiling point of water as 100 degrees.

Chemical reaction When two or more substances mix together and change their form to make a new substance.

Condensed Cooled down and changed back from a vapour or a gas into a solid or liquid.

Conduction When heat is passed through a material by the particles inside it, or from the particles of one material to those of another material touching it.

Electricity A kind of energy that makes some of the particles inside a material flow in one direction.

Evaporation A change from a solid or liquid into a vapour.

Filament The thin, tightly-wound piece of wire inside a bulb that glows when electricity passes through it.

Friction When materials that are rubbed together catch on each other and become warm.

Gases Materials, such as natural gas and air, that are usually colourless and have particles which are very loosely bound together.

Heat energy The kind of energy that raises the temperature of a material.

Humidity The dampness of the air.

Kelvin The temperature scale, invented by William Kelvin, that takes as its starting point the temperature at which all materials have become solids.

Insulator A material that does not allow heat (or electricity or sound) to pass through it.

Lens A piece of glass or perspex that bends light which is passing through it. Some lenses direct light rays to meet at a point and others scatter rays in different directions.

Liquid A material, such as water, that has particles bound together less closely than those of a solid, but closer than those of a gas.

Meteorite A piece of rock or metal that has entered the earth's atmosphere, where friction makes it burn up.

Radiate To give out into the air.

Reflect To send something such as light or heat back again.

Solid A material, such as wood or plastic, that has particles bound tightly together so that it has a definite shape.

Thermometers Instruments that measure temperature.

Vacuum An area where there are no solids, liquids or gases.

Vapour A material that has evaporated so that its particles are mixed with the air as a gas. Sometimes a condensed vapour can be seen as clouds or smoke.

Books to read

Pocket Book of Science by Robin Kerrod (Kingfisher, 1990)

Cambridge Illustrated Dictionary for the Young Scientist by Jeanne Stone (Cambridge, 1985)

Energy in Primary Schools Unit 6: Heat (Department of Energy)

Heat by Joy Richardson (Franklin Watts, 1992)

Heating and Cooling by David Crystal and John Foster (Hodder and Stoughton, 1991)

How Things Work: Heat by Andrew Dunn (Wayland, 1992)

Heat by Chris Carter (Heinemann, 1991)

Physics for every kid: 101 easy experiments in motion, heat, light, machines and sound by Janice Vancleave (Wiley, 1991)

Notes for parents and teachers

Pages 4-5 These activities show the need for an objective measure of temperature. Make sure that the water is no more than hand-hot. The most useful thermometers to use for these activities are -10°C to 60°C room thermometers. However, these will shatter at temperatures of above 60° C, so you will also need to have thermometers which cover the range -10°C to 110°C. These are longer, more expensive and rather fragile, so care is needed.

Pages 6-7 The first home-made thermometer relies on the expansion of liquid as it warms up. The second half-full thermometer is more sensitive since it relies to a large extent on the expansion of the air in the bottle. Neither is accurate.

The balloon shows that warm air takes up more space than cold air. It is the space between the air particles, not the particles themselves, which expands.

Pages 8-9 Metals are much the best conductors of heat. They have free electrons which carry the heat rapidly. Insulators have no free electrons. They conduct heat through passing on the vibration of their atoms.

Metals feel colder than wood and plastic because they conduct heat away from your hand. They are not really colder than other materials. Similarly polystyrene feels warm not because it is warm, but because it conducts heat so badly that hardly any of your hand's heat is taken away.

Pages 10-11 The pie plate turns because hot air above the candle flames rises and pushes against the fins cut in the plate. The fins should be large and evenly spaced.

Water, like all other materials, contracts as it gets colder until it reaches the temperature of 4°C. At that temperature it is at its most dense and so sinks to the bottom of ponds and lakes. Below 4°C, water expands until it reaches 0°C, when it is at its greatest volume. If it did not do this, warmer water would not sink, and nothing could survive in ponds in freezing weather.

Pages 12-13 The lens focuses the sun's heat and light so that it is concentrated in a small area. Black print absorbs heat better than white paper so it is scorched more easily.

The solar cooker works by concentrating the sun's heat as a focus point in the way that a satellite dish concentrates radio waves at the aerial in the centre.

Pages 14-15 Matt black objects absorb heat most effectively and shiny silver objects absorb heat least of all.

Water absorbs heat very well, better in fact than the solid materials which make up the rocks of the land.

Pages 16-17 Vacuum flasks are just as good at stopping the heat from a warm room melting ice as they are at keeping drinks hot.

Large objects stay warm longer than small ones. This is because they have a small surface area compared with their mass. In this activity only half fill the bottles, to keep them stable.

Pages 18-19 Water needs heat energy for it to change into water vapour. The damp cloth covering the milk bottle takes some of this heat away from the glass of the bottle, and cools it. Wind and sun both speed up evaporation, so in these conditions there will be a greater difference between the temperatures of the bottles.

The air blown by fans is usually at the same temperature as the surroundings. We feel cooler under a fan because the breeze helps water to evaporate more quickly off our skin.

Pages 20-21 Compost heaps can reach very high temperatures. The heat is generated by the bacteria, as they decompose the garden waste, in the same way that heat is produced by our own bodies. When we exercise, we produce even more heat than usual.

Page 22-3 Hardwood gives the best results with this activity. Although it is easy to make the end of the dowel hot, it is very difficult to create enough heat to start a fire.

Pages 24-5 This activity gives wonderfully unexpected results, as the temperature drops below freezing. Look out also for the increased condensation on the outside of the container. If you are lucky this condensation will change to ice. Freezing mixtures similar to this were used to make conditions cold enough for the first ice-creams.

The ice cubes on the materials which conduct heat the best will melt first.

Pages 26-7 If you heat the ice slowly and stir, the temperature should remain just above freezing before all the ice melts. However, it may creep up to 3° or 4°C.

Pages 28-9 Cooking makes a good finale to investigating heat, because it demonstrates much of what has been discovered and you can eat the results!

Index

Answer to the question on p.27: water will boil at **85° C.**